Everything I Know About
Stress Management
I Got From Elijah

By Dr. Philip Oldfield

Dedication

I would like to dedicate this book to Helen my wife and best friend who has had the misfortune of having to put up with my strange ways, and sense of humour for over 30 years. She has always been there for me during both the good and the rough times, and we are more friends now than we've ever been.

Table of Contents

Chapters

1. Introduction

I had obviously spent too long working for large corporations and the politics that involves. Certainly in my time I've seen quite a few people "burnout" for one reason or another. In fact nearly 20 years ago I think the same happened to me, although I didn't realize it at the time. I have always intended to write a book, outlining practical ways on how to help yourself and others before everything can get so out of control. Also, when I've been down, and it happens quite a bit, people just don't know how to respond, and in many cases made my situation worse.

Yep! ...... I've written a chapter on that too.

Anyway enough about me; we are going to go back in time to the year 860 BC. It's about a man who, if he was alive today would certainly be a candidate for the Special Forces. He was physically fit and psychologically tough; working comfortably all on his own behind enemy lines he would have made a very good operative; and yet given the right circumstances he had a nervous break-down. That tells me, that no one is immune; we can all fall victim given the right conditions. Therefore we need to observe quickly what is happening in our lives at an early stage, and take the appropriate action before it gets completely out of control.

So in "Everything I know about stress management I got from Elijah" we are going to look at those conditions that contribute to a nervous break-down situation, and the restoration processes that need to take place; as well as an understanding of the man himself. All of which took place approximately 2870 years ago.

Always remember if all else fails, go to the maker's manual:

(The Bible, Deut 11:16-17 and 1Kings 17:1 – 19:21). Bible verses will appropriately paraphrased not quoted. However, Biblical references will be indicated for your information.

This is the first in a series of books that I intend to publish, covering a variety of different but relevant topics. Also, the chapter "About the Author" will change with each book, so you don't get bored reading the same thing over and over again.

2.   About the Author

Now if you were to go on my Linkedin page you would read the following about me:

Philip R. Oldfield obtained his D.Phil. in 1982. The subject of his research was "Proteolytic Control and Rheumatoid Disease". In 1986 he was given the Baker Award for his work on Digoxin-Like-Immunoreactive-Substances. He has over 25 years experience in service to the pharmaceutical and biopharmaceutical industry specializing in ligand binding assay techniques including hybridization assays. He is currently President and CEO of his own consulting company. Dr Oldfield has a keen interest in forensic science and is an Associate Member of the Royal College of Pathologists, a Fellow of the Royal Society of Chemistry, and a Member of the American Association of Pharmaceutical Scientists, (is currently the Past Chair of the Ligand Binding Assay Bioanalytical Focus Group). In addition he likes to maintain a link with the local universities, and has been involved in supervising postgraduate students, as well the occasional lecture. He is currently involved as a committee member to organize symposia and workshops as part of the Drug Development Program Course at the University of McGill.

However if you want to know how I view myself read on:

What can I say? From the beginning I was born on the 11th of July at the Hammersmith Hospital London UK. Don't bother working out my age just surprise me with a present. In my early years from the day I was born I was sick with breathing problems. So my parents allowed me to take up indoor activities (big mistake).

My first activity was electronics; in fact I started my own business at the age of 8. My mum eventually, bands me from continuing after been shocked on several occasions. So they got me a chemistry set (even bigger mistake). I made a chlorine generator in the bath in order to eliminate an infestation of bed bugs. I think, I collapsed and was carried outside (the bugs in question were still there). When I was 19 years old I worked at the Hammersmith Hospital as a student technician in the Clinical Chemistry department. The Consultant remembered the day I was born and said that I was very sick; some people think I still am. From then on I decided that I wanted to become a scientist, and ended up with lots of letters after my name. With regards to my chemistry skills, I eventually became a Fellow of the Royal Society of Chemistry (I didn't tell them about my experiments when I was younger). I'm distracted by shiny obj..........

.......Umm! Now where was I... of course love traveling, and horse riding (I've been told I got nice hindquarters), and was involved with the Riding for the Disabled Association. I'm married to Helen and have two grown up children Monica and Benjamin. I'm not scared of bugs unless I see half of one in my food, Yep! That's happened. I believe in the supernatural hence why I am a Christian. I'm not superstitious; I have 13 Chapters in this book; and I just hate saying good-bye....Hi.

3.   *What a place to live*

Elijah was a Tishbite from Thisbe a town in that country in Gilead. He was referred to on many occasions as Elijah the Tishbite (pioneer). Well, you have to be tough to be a pioneer; Gilead means rocky, so even the terrain he lived in was rough. Therefore, as a child he learnt the art of living in this rocky wilderness. This meant that, as he grew up, he became physically fit and psychologically tough; able to survive a variety of adverse situations. At that time Israel's official religion was Baal, so it was also very tough if you happened to believe in the LORD.

Baal worship must be the most degraded religion ever invented, and the Baal worship introduced into Israel at that time was the worst of all, and deemed evil, by all other pagans in the known region. When the Romans who are hardly good examples of virtue themselves; arrived in Carthage, and encountered Baal worship for the first time, even they were utterly grossed out by it. You see, Baal worship went hand in hand with sex, violence, murderous blood lust, and unspeakable cruelty, and I mean unspeakable. Imagine your worst horror movie incorporating all of the above multiplied by at least ten that would be Baal worship. Take it from me, I've read some of their poetry; I agree with the Romans, it is utterly gross. Probably just as well, if not indeed planned, that Elijah was brought up in the mountainous terrain in a settlement called Thisbe out in the wilderness, and away from 'civilization'.

4.   To the unsung heroes

You can tell a lot from a man by his name, at least in those days. You see, his name was Elijah which means "the God in whom I stand whose specific name is Jehovah (The LORD)". You may think, no big deal, until you consider that the vast majority of the people in the land including Ahab the King Israel worshipped the false god Baal; Yep! It was the official religion in Israel during this time; trust Queen Jezebel to lead the King of Israel astray. So either his parents didn't like him, or that his parents were true believers in the LORD, and gave him this wonderful name "Elijah" and home schooled him accordingly. I don't think they had high schools at that time, but if they did, he would be in the minority and they would make fun of his name, or try to kill him. I would have to say that Elijah's parents were believers in the LORD because of what is going to happen in the next chapter, and are the unsung heroes in the Bible. Not once were they mentioned, and yet without them Elijah would not have been the man of God and the great prophet for that special moment in history. You see, by this time Elijah had a good grounding in the teachings of the LORD, and I might add had a good relationship with God. Therefore he was also spiritually strong; and had hope; a very important safety factor in the battle against depression and/or a nervous break-down. Not to mention that his father would have taught him all the necessary survival skills.

5.   That's awfully brave!

So what happened that day? As every good believer, he would have read the Holy Scriptures which at the time would have been the first 5 books of the Bible and of course he would also pray. On that very day the scroll would have open at Deuteronomy chapter 11 verses 16-17, so he would have read:

Deut 11:v16 to 17:   Be careful that you are not deceived and follow after other gods; serving and worshiping them. At that time the LORD's anger will be against you. There will be no rain, and will have famine in the land that the LORD gave you.

As I mentioned before, the official religion at the time was Baal, introduced by the King of Israel; which would come under the category of serving other gods and worshiping them. So reading that passage and knowing Israel's current situation; Elijah being inspired by the LORD went to see King Ahab in his ivory place in Samaria:

1Kings 17:v1: Elijah the Tishbite, said to King Ahab, As the LORD lives in whom I stand, there will be no rain until I say so.

He then walks straight out of the palace fully intact and very much alive. That's awfully brave! Imagine it, would you go and do something like that, even if the LORD was to tell you? Elijah was certainly courageous, not the kind of person you would expect to have a nervous break-down.

Also, something else that would otherwise go unnoticed is that the passage referred to him as: "Elijah the Tishbite", whereas I would have expected: "Elijah from Thisbe" which would be the norm. Therefore to translate; the passage actually says "Elijah the Pioneer", or the 21st century equivalent "Elijah the mountain man". I just find that interesting, because it is more of a description of the man himself, as opposed to where he came from.

6.   Fire in the hole!

Over 3 years had passed and Elijah meets up with
King Ahab again, this time with challenge:

1Kings 18:v17 to 24:   Over three years had past
when Ahab saw Elijah again and said there you are,
the trouble maker in Israel. Elijah told King Ahab in no
uncertain terms that he had brought the trouble upon
himself and Israel by going against the LORD's
commandments; serving and worshiping the false god
Baal. He then told Ahab to gather all the people of
Israel; to include the 450 prophets of Baal as well as
the 400 prophets of Asherah who eat at Jezebel's
table; to meet him at Mount Carmel. When the
multitudes were gathered, Elijah said to them, you
need to choose between the LORD and Baal, all of the
people were silent, and then he gave them a
challenge. Elijah was to prepare a bullock for
sacrifice, and the 850 prophets of Baal and Asherah
were to do the same. So here's the deal; the prophets
of Baal and Asherah will call upon their god, Elijah will
then call upon the LORD, and whoever answers by
fire and consumes the sacrifice is the one and only
true God. All of the people said: Yep! That sounds
good to us.

Now Baal was a god of the weather; well he didn't
have much luck over the past three years. He was
also the god of fire; their sacrifices would go up in
flames apparently all by itself. However, what was not
widely known was that there was "fire in the hole!"
Yep! There would be a tunnel in which one of the Baal

prophets would crawl through and light the fire from below setting the sacrifice alight. Therefore when Elijah makes his challenge to the Baal prophets as well as those who followed the religion of Asherah, they could not refuse, and it sounded good to the people who worshipped Baal because normally their sacrifices did go up in flames all by itself. Now which god was going to be the "God of Fire" Baal or the LORD? The location for the showdown was perfect, solid limestone; try digging a tunnel out of that in a hurry. So what happened, the 450 Baal and 400 Asherah prophets went first and started early. Well nothing happen, no fire in the hole, in fact there was no hole. So they started to cut themselves and go into frenzy; still nothing happened. Elijah would be taunting them while he eats his lunch. What he actually said to them would probably lead to his excommunication from your average church.

During this time Elijah built a simple alter, placed the sacrifice, poured water on the sacrifice, dug ditches and filled them with water. In fact it seemed as if he was sabotaging his own efforts. What he was actually doing was nothing less than a demonstration of his faith in the LORD and showing to world that there were no tricks involved when it came to the LORD's sacrifice. Elijah then waited for the time of the evening sacrifice, fire came down from heaven as planned, boiled up the water in the ditches and completely burnt up the sacrifice. Game over!

Having demonstrated that the LORD was the true God; all of the Baal and Asherah prophets were put to death by the rest of the people. The rain came on the land after at least three years of drought, and Elijah outran Ahab's chariot in a marathon all the way to Jezreel. So here's a man who on his own faces 850 false prophets, has an exceptional trust in his God, and can outrun a chariot in a marathon. He doesn't seem to me to be the kind of person you would expect to have a nervous break-down.

7. *The wicked witch of the Middle East*

King Ahab had a wife, her name was Jezebel and she definitely had control over King Ahab big time. Jezebel originally came from Sidonia where her name means "primrose"; in Hebrew the word means "a dung pile". So you could say that she was very attractive on the outside, which by the way she was; and I don't really need to say what she was on the inside. Nowadays her name is such that parents in their right mind would never call their daughters Jezebel. In the dictionary this name is defined as an offensive term for a woman who is sexually immoral or manipulative. If by chance you happen to have the name Jezebel; don't feel bad about it or down, it's up to you to determine what's on the inside. After all, people spend a lot of time on their outward appearances; it's about time we looked on the inside. At the time of Elijah she was "The Wicked Witch of the Middle East". Witchcraft is defined in a book that I read as the art of control through manipulation, intimidation, and domination; and let me tell you, she was an expert. There is an old saying that goes: "sticks and stones my break my bones but words will never harm me"; that saying could not be further from the truth. Words are very powerful they can make peace or start wars, and we all take them to heart. When I was 13 years old and I wanted to take up the biology at school; the Head of Biology told me in no uncertain terms that I "would never get into any form of higher education".

Yep! That hurt; and not only that, I believed it for years. It wasn't until I was at University helping other people with their biology assignments when it occurred to me how damaging such false statements are. I was very fortunate that I had a consultant and two professors at the Royal Postgraduate Medical School where I worked as a Technician who spent time with me, and eventually encouraged me to go to University. To show that I'm not sexist; the Head of Biology in the high school I attended was a man. Now let's get back to Jezebel.

Jezebel, this crafty and unscrupulous woman came from a long line of tyrants. Her father Ethbaal (I'm with Baal) King of Sidon, murdered his brothers in order to get to the throne. King Ahab had no idea what he was letting himself in for. You could say that he was the puppet, and she was pulling the strings. King Ahab was weak enough to be controlled by his wife, and not only that, she would act on his behalf without him even being aware of it. She was the one who instigated killing off of the LORD's prophets during that time, which by the way was also another reason why Elijah was so brave. It seemed that her sole objective was to establish Baal and Asherah worship as the only religion in Israel, by effectively killing off the opposition. Witchcraft is not broomsticks and dancing round a fire naked, it is far worse, and perhaps more widespread than we think.

8.   *Under the tree of despair*

Back to Elijah; OK there was the victory at Mount Carmel all the false prophets were dead, and he even beat Ahab's chariot back to Jezreel. King Ahab goes and sulks to his wife:

1Kings 19:v1:   Ahab told Jezebel what Elijah had done and also how he had killed all of the prophets with the sword.

Actually, it was not Elijah who killed the prophets of Baal and Asherah but the people of Israel. Now just see what Jezebel does:

1Kings 19:v2:   Jezebel filled with anger sent a messenger to Elijah, promising to kill him in the same way that her prophets were killed within 24 hours.

Elijah gets this message, and runs for his life, and becomes an emotional wreck:

1Kings 19:v3 to 4: When Elijah heard the message, he ran for his life to Beersheba which at that time belonged to Judah. Elijah left his servant there and walked on for another day in the wilderness, sat down under a juniper tree wishing for death, asked the LORD to take away his life, asserting that he was no better than anyone else in Israel.

Not the Elijah we have seen in the previous chapters. So what happened; let us focus on what is going on with Elijah. He is mentally and physically exhausted, just think about it; what happened during the entire day.   For hours on his own he faced 850 false prophets, trusting the whole time in the LORD his God. Runs a marathon and beats King Ahab's Chariot to the finish line. I would say that he was absolutely pooped! All it took was a few words from Jezebel's messenger to send him over the edge. Then to top it all, he ran for his life all the way to Beersheba about 100 miles; leaves his servant there.   He then continues his journey into the wilderness for another day. Well if he wasn't pooped out after the marathon, he was now.   By this time he also felt alone and abandoned, having lost sight of God and without hope. With all of the safety factors gone, and all of the conditions in place there was nothing he could do. It doesn't matter how strong you are, when these factors come into play, there is no avoiding a nervous break-down; it will happen.

So please, never ever consider that a person is weak because they had a "burnout".

9.   Are you a Goodie-Two-Shoes or an Angel?

Don't you hate it when you're depressed, feeling down, and concerned about the future; when some goes up to you and says: "I would like to hear all about it?" And when you do, they then say: "Don't worry about it." Or "Worry is a SIN", and then have a go at you, making the assertion that you must have done something wrong for all of these misfortunes to have happened. Worst of all, a person goes up to you and asks: "how are you?" And when you tell them, they just turn and walk the other way, and totally ignore you. Yep! That's happened to me; all of the above. What is really funny is that they actually think they're doing good; when in fact it could not be further from the truth.

In this chapter we are going to find out what an Angel would do:

1Kings 19:v5 to 7: As Elijah slept under the juniper tree and angel of the LORD touched him and said get up and eat. The angel provided a cake baked on coals and jar of water to drink. After Elijah ate the food and drank the water, the angel told him to sleep. The angel came back a second time and told him to get up and eat because the journey had just physically drained him.

Unlike us humans, the LORD is very practical and sent an angel to see that his physical needs were met; that is food and drink, and a good night's sleep. It makes perfect sense; if you want to break a person the first thing you would do is deprive them food, drink, and sleep. Therefore, in order to restore a person the converse also has to be true. Remember he was physically weak at the time he reached Jezreel, and then running for his life; it was at lease another 100 miles before he reached Beersheba, and then a day's journey before he finally reached the juniper tree. I would say after all of that he was definitely pooped and messed up.

What do I mean by an "Angel"? In this case it means treating someone the way you would like to be treated, a question not very often asked. The last thing you need is someone who wants to get into an in depth discussion to instantly fix your problems. What really communicates is when I come across a person who really cares for me. Not there to fix my problems, but just to get alongside me as a friend. Going out for dinner "remember food and drink", and just hanging out with some good friend's "good food good company". They don't even need to say a word, just being with them and enjoying the moment. Yep! That would do it for me.

So please! Don't be a "Goodie-Two-Shoes"; be an "Angel"!

10. Just chilling out

This is where I demonstrate my misunderstanding. Here's the situation, I'm in my 30's working for a big corporation living in a small English Village. Over the weekend I took a walk along the street to do some shopping and have lunch at the local pub with my family. It suddenly occurred to me, all of these old men on the sidewalk sitting on their chairs just looking at the street and people walking by. I remember thinking to myself; "what a waste of time!" Over 20 years later, I'm living in Canada, sitting down on a chair just looking at the yachts, the trees, the grass, the little animals; and thinking to myself; "what a hypocrite!" As I saw the younger people looking at me, probably thinking the same thing I did 20 years earlier.

I have learnt over the years that life is unnaturally going at a pace far quicker than we can absorb. What I mean is this; we need time just to chill-out, forget about work, finances, cell-phone, computer, Facebook, whatever; and just take in the moment. It is all part of the restoration process, to hear the sound yachts make with their metal bits (you can tell I'm not into sailing), the wind blowing through the trees, seeing the squirrels running about, looking at me and thinking: "what a waste of time, he should be collecting nuts like the rest of us!". Chilling out is actually good for emotional well being; at least that's my experience.

Now let's get back to Elijah. The angel ensured that he had enough to eat and drink and enough sleep:

1Kings 19:v7 to 8: The angel came a second time and told him to get up and eat because the journey had just physically drained him. Elijah now strengthened by the food got up and took a journey taking forty days and forty nights to Mount Horeb to meet with God.

When Elijah's physical strength was restored, God wanted him to take a walk for 40 days. The distance was no big deal, literally a walk in the park. However, during those 40 days he was taking in the moment, relaxing, and slowly but surely becoming increasingly emotionally stable. Note that the physical restoration comes first.

If you are not eating and sleeping properly, there is no way that you are going to be restored emotionally.

11. A gentle whisper

At first glance it seemed strange that the LORD didn't speak to and restore Elijah at the Juniper tree. After all it would have saved 42 days. However, having thought about it; it was necessary, I mean, why disagree with God?

1Kings 19:v8 to 18: Elijah now strengthened by the food got up and took a journey taking forty days and forty nights to Mount Horeb to meet with God. He went into a cave and stayed there, and then the LORD spoke into his thoughts, why are you here? Elijah then proceeded to pour out his heart saying how faithful he was, and what the rest of Israel did by destroying the LORD's alters and killing LORD's prophets. If that wasn't enough, I'm the only one left and they are after me too. The LORD said go and stand upon the mountain. The LORD passed by, a great and strong wind that shook the mountain, but the LORD was not in the wind. After the wind came an earthquake; but the LORD was not in the earthquake. After the earthquake came fire; but the LORD was not in the fire. Then there was a small still voice, as soon as he heard it he covered his face and went out to the entrance of the cave. A voice said to him, why are you here? Elijah again poured out his heart saying how faithful he was, and what the rest of Israel did by destroying the LORD's alters and killing LORD's prophets. If that wasn't enough, I'm the only one left and they are after me too. The LORD then said Elijah, now go back to the desert of Damascus and anoint Hazael to be King of Syria. Also anoint Jehu son of Nimshi King of Israel, and Elisha son of Shaphat from Abel Meholah to succeed you as prophet. Jehu shall put to death anyone who escapes Hazael, and Elisha shall put to death anyone who escapes Jehu. Elijah, don't you realize that I had reserved for myself seven thousand people in Israel who have remained faithful, and have not bowed down to that false god Baal or kissed his image.

There is an order in which things have to be done. First of all restoring the person's physical strength, this also includes getting a good night's sleep; that's where the angel came in. Second was to be restored emotionally, that was where the walk and chilling out came in. This is very often missed out, we do need to have time on our own without distractions to think things through; there's just too much going on nowadays. Now what happens is what I would like to call spiritual restoration. Something very interesting happens. Elijah actually repeats himself; once when the word of the LORD came to him, and then there was that small still voice when he actually met with God. Notice that the LORD did not tell him off, or rebuke him, but gave him another job to do, and encouraged him. At that point Elijah knew that he would never feel alone or abandoned ever again. In addition, God had renewed his vision, a sense of destiny, and realized that he was never alone in the first place.

Remember, God was not in the strong wind, or in the earthquake, or in the fire; God was in that small still voice that speaks into our hearts saying "I love you."

The LORD always brings hope to anyone who listens; anyone! Even you ☺

12.   Forever changed

When you go through a "burnout" or nervous break-down, you're never quite the same person, and that's OK.   The important thing is where do we go from here? Being hurt by other people can very easily lead to bitterness.   Sure you sort of recover, but in the process you are slowly but surely destroying yourself, while the person who you have not forgiven from the heart is perfectly unaware of what's going on. In fact the person you are holding a grudge against may well already be dead. On the positive side we can learn from our experiences.   Remember when I was told that I would never get into any form of higher education. Well, my big lesson is that I would never go up to anyone and say you cannot achieve an objective, no matter what it is. However, what I will do is to outline carefully what is required and take the conversation from there.

I think over the years I have become more of an encourager. It's great to be involved in building other people up, and in a real way you can share in their success. I've also learnt to have a thankful heart. We all have something to be thankful for, but in the society in which we live; people have been conditioned to focus on what they don't have. Thankful people tend not to complain, and they are also a lot happier for it. The take home message is and face up to it; bad things do happen to good people.

It's not what happened that's going to determine the outcome so much as how we deal with it.

13. It's all up to you

The factors contributing to stress are:

A need for food and drink

A lack of sleep

Emotional instability

Lack of support (You're on your own)

When all the above factors come into play, as we have seen it doesn't matter how strong you are; a burnout is inevitable. Out of all of these it is the lack of support that can be the most damaging. If you feel that you are not being supported you must talk about it before you get stressed out. Try to cultivate good friendships; someone you can turn to, and choose your friends carefully. Try to associate with people who make you feel good and at ease; and don't put you down all the time. Mentoring is good for obtaining advice and for personal development, be it character or career. Very often the mentor and mentee become the best of friends and the advice goes both ways. In our society developing good friendships is probably more difficult now than it's ever been. Friendships cannot be forged over the internet, nothing can replace personal contact either socially or working together.

Over work

Unforeseen problems

Conflict

Lack of support

Over work:

First of all be objective and set your priorities, not everything can be done at once, even if your boss wants it that way. It's probably an indication that your boss doesn't understand what the task involves. Don't panic; alternatively don't ignore it. Assess the resources available, and plan your time effectively, this also provides proof that you are doing the best you can with the available resources; not only that, but that you are also demonstrating a high level of efficiency. You may also need to reassess your training needs. Feel free to talk about any work related or other stress; and if for some reason you cannot communicate this with your boss; this is where a good friend or mentor comes in.

Unforeseen problems:

Although there is some overlap between this and over work, in this case we are talking about unexpected events in which you would need to reassess and plan your schedule. First of all ensure that adequate resources are available to cope with the issue, communicate with the people who can make a difference i.e. your boss or supervisor, and agree on a plan of action. It is very important not to go into a panic, it's infective and ineffective, indicative of losing control.

Conflict:

Yep! That's a big one! Be sure not to allow your emotions to speak for you, in other words act don't react, that takes planning. Which mean that you don't have to respond at the time; God gave us two ears but only one mouth. We all need to be good listeners' try to see where the other person is coming from. Deal with the issues only and don't insult the person you are in conflict with; in other words you are to be professional, so keep focused. In the end it will be you that would look good, don't look for a fight, but always be prepared just in case.

Maintaining a balance:

Now I would like to provide more of a practical guide. Of course people talk about having a balanced life, and it means different things to different people, and that's OK. We all need to find our own balance; personally I'm more of a couch potato person. First of all look after yourself, remember to eat, drink and have a good night's sleep especially when you are exhausted. If you are not exhausted physically but are tending to eat too much, then actually some exercise would do you good, we can all take a walk and chill-out. Some people might find it difficult to forget about work when they get home. Well, if you are one of those people, then try this out; get into a change of clothes when you get home from work. It's amazing how that works!

What I also find useful, remember me sitting down on a chair watching the yachts and life go by, taking in the moment. It's at times like these when you can decide what kind of person you would like to be; instead of being driven by circumstances having no control of how you are going to end up; it's very subtle. So as you would have guessed already I think that a sense of humour is essential, laughter is a great stress reliever; also be real, be yourself. I'm not exactly the most quiet of people. For years I tried my best to be quiet; didn't work! I'm now happy the way I am, and with my lot in life. In fact, I've become very thankful even for the slightest things, and I never, or at least hardly ever focus on what I don't have. It really is a good place to be.

Lack of support:

Getting back to Elijah, it was 850:1 (with God). Although I have already covered lack of support, there is another aspect.

This is the story of how I died:

From the age of about 11, when I woke up one morning healed from a lung condition I had from birth, I've always been looking for a purpose in life, to know the reason why!

During the late 70's, I was at University, and managed through no fault of my own to surround myself with people called Christians. There was me saying "Save starving lions - Become a Christian", just to rattle their cages (not the lions). One day a friend of mine named Mike spoke to me very clearly about what Christianity was all about. The first thing he said is that we are all created to have a personal relationship with God, without God we just feel empty inside, no matter how much we have materially. I knew inside that was true. So why doesn't everyone have God in their lives?

The answer was quite simple, it's because we don't want to. We want to live our lives the way we want; we are in complete control. He proceeded to explain to me that it was this very attitude and rejection of God is what the Bible calls Sin and everyone of us are affected. So being a Christian doesn't mean that I'm better than anyone else, in fact the opposite is true; at some point I realized my need for God. There are also consequences; Sin equates to Death. We are not only considering natural death which happens to all of us, but of spiritual death. That is, a life without God, an eternity in the mist of absolute evil (i.e. your worst nightmare multiplexed by infinity).

God loves us and therefore gave his only Son Jesus Christ, so that anyone who believes in Him will not perish but have eternal life with God. I was then told that it's wasn't enough just to know this.

By the time Mike and other people told me this, over a period of at least 6 months, another Christian friend of mine named Monica (ok so I named my daughter after her), who I met on a train, enabled me to see what I actually believed. That Jesus Christ did live on the earth lived a perfect life, died and rose from the dead. I knew at this point I had a choice to make.

In the end I said just a simple prayer asking Jesus to "come into my life as my Lord and Savior and to make me into the kind of person He wanted me to be". I didn't feel any different except for the peace I felt knowing I made the right choice, and more than thirty years later, I still believe that. It's not been easy, and it still isn't, but its well worth it.

I don't know what the future holds, but I know who holds my future. I know that "God will never leave me or forsake me".

This is the story of how I died

I have died with Christ and no longer live for myself, but Christ lives in me, allowing me to follow His plan for my life. Therefore the life I live is by trusting in God who has planned only good for me since the beginning of time. Because God loves me and gave himself for me.

An illustration from the book "The History of the Church & Parish of St. Mary's on the Hill Chester" Printed by Love & Wyman Ltd. London 1898.

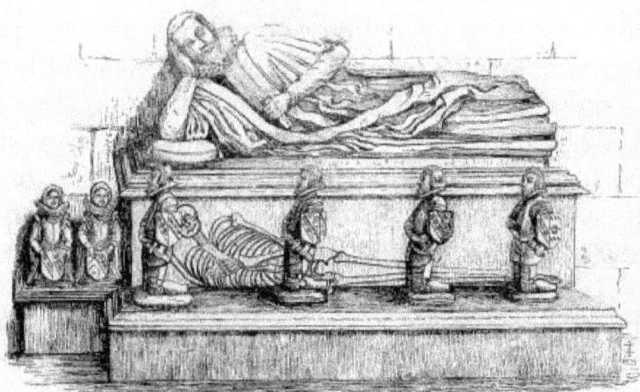

MONUMENT TO PHILIP OLDFIELD, Esq.

If you were go to a church called St. Mary's on the Hill in Chester England; it's a great place to visit, you will find in St. Catherine's chapel the sarcophagus of Philip Oldfield who died on 15th December 1616 aged 75. The resemblance is remarkable, fantastic sense of humour, and his wife's name was Helen.

Here is Philip Oldfield standing next to the sarcophagus of Philip Oldfield. Earlier I had mentioned that I'm a "couch potato"; is that a remote he has in his hand? Also, I'm left handed; take a closer look. You would never want to be left handed in the 1600's.

I wonder if there's such a thing as time travel?

www.ingramcontent.com/pod-product-compliance
Lightning Source LLC
Chambersburg PA
CBHW022350040426
42449CB00006B/801